Leaving Abuse Behind

SARAH DANIEL

AUBURN HOUSE

To all who seek to know the truth
And all who strive to heal

Published in 1995 by
Auburn House,
A division of Salmon Publishing Ltd,
Upper Fairhill, Galway

A catalogue record for this book is available from the British Library.

ISBN 1 897648 38 3

Cover batik by Noirín Mooney
Cover design by Poolbeg Group Services Ltd
Set by Poolbeg Group Services Ltd in Garamond 11/14
Printed by Colour Books, Baldoyle, Dublin 13.

Contents

Acknowledgements

The obvious people to thank first for the existence of this book are my family, without whose contributions to my life the writing of this book would have been unnecessary! And in fact, this book came about because of an incomplete confrontation with someone in my family. I was entering the departure lounge at New York's Kennedy Airport on my way to Ireland, when I spied sitting in the front row the one living relative whom I would prefer never to see again, with spouse, whom I would also prefer never to see again.

This relative sodomised me when I was a child, off and on for about two years. A year after the memories of the sodomy returned, I decided I couldn't continue to pretend that everything was fine and that nothing had happened. Either we had to get the issue out in the open, discuss it and get on with our lives, or I had to stop behaving as if all was well. I initiated a confrontation by letter with this relative. His response was negative and abusive. I wrote back to repeat that I couldn't continue to pretend to keep up the family relationship, and would not be writing him again. One more letter arrived from him, which I did not reply to. Four years went by with no contact. It had been ten since I had seen him or his wife.

When I suddenly saw them in the flesh, it was as if I were in terrible danger. I was eight years old again, and bound to do whatever my larger and more powerful relative insisted that I do. I had just told my mother what he did, and she said it was all my fault. Part of me was instantly returned to some of the worst scenes of my childhood. I wanted to disappear. I wanted to hide. I wanted, at all costs, to avoid being seen by them.

I was able through my husband's intervention to avoid running into them on the way into the plane. Then I spent five hours in agony. I was fearful, curious about what they were doing there, morbidly fascinated by them and by my own reactions, appalled at being transported back to a terrible time, this time unprotected by loss of memory or the convenient atmosphere of shared denial. I was terrified that I would see them again at Shannon and have to interact with them.

About an hour out of Shannon, a change came over me. I decided not to take any extraordinary measures to avoid these relatives. After all, I was the one who had the grievance. I was the one who could cause trouble if I had to. If they spoke to me, I could just be rude. (I had never been allowed to be rude to these people. I had been brought up to accept anything they had to dish out, no matter how offensive.)

As we made our way toward the exit of the plane at Shannon, my ex–in–law happened (you know how that goes) to turn around and look straight at me. I felt as though 1,000 volts of electricity shot through me, rooting me to the floor. I looked at this person for about 30 seconds, then calmly averted my gaze and went forward in the line without glancing at them again. It wasn't much as confrontations go, but for the first time in my life I did what I had always wanted to – cut them dead.

All week, I was exhilarated, amused, amazed at the encounter. My energy was good, my health improved. For the time at least I lost my fear and became very outgoing. One day during that visit my friend Brian Mooney, of the Burren Perfumery, asked one of his typically searching questions. "How do you actually get

OVER something like what happened to you?" he asked.

"Well," said I, "The first thing you have to do is to remember what happened. Then you have to tell somebody." And I went on like that for some time. "Sarah," said my husband, "You're writing a book!"

When we returned to America I walked in the door, put down my suitcase, turned on the computer and started the book. After I finished it, it sat in the computer for two years before I had any idea what to do with such a small book about abuse.

By that time I had moved to Ireland and had met Jessie Lendennie, of Auburn House. She suggested that my book be published as is, no matter how short. In fact, she thought that the concise writing might help people. I began to give the manuscript to people to read, and found out that Jessie and my husband were correct. The book helps people.

I would like to thank everybody concerned with Auburn House for their excellent assistance and their good humour. I would like to thank Noirin Mooney for her sensitive reading of the manuscript and for her lovely batiks. Thanks also go to Ivor Browne for his support and his extremely helpful suggestions about the text.

I want to thank Harvey Wasserman for all the years of companionship and help. Without his steadfast love I don't think I would have survived everything I had to go through to come to this moment, book or no book.

And, of course – as I said at the beginning – acknowledgements go also to my family. They began it all. I am completing it in my own way.

Sarah Daniel
February, 1995

Preface

From the very first page this book is clear and concise. The approach is open and calm, facing without any equivocation, what anyone who has been abused and traumatised in their childhood has to go through, with all the pain and suffering which this involves, if they are to be healed.

It is interesting that although Sarah Daniel doesn't have the understanding of how overwhelming traumatic experience is blocked in its pathway through the primitive brain, the stages of healing which she describes are virtually identical with those which I have found in dealing with many cases of sexual abuse and childhood trauma.

My drawing attention to this is in no sense meant as a criticism of the author for I would not expect her to be familiar with the fairly recent developments in neurophysiology which have taken place over the past thirty or forty years. But it is now well established that for any experience to be processed into long term memory the information has to be worked through the primitive brain (the limbic system – specifically the hippocampus). This is the ancient part of the brain which we share with other mammals – what

Arthur Koestler referred to as "the horse brain". Although we are not normally conscious of most of its workings the limbic system still manages most of the functions which enable us to survive – maintenance of consciousness, cardiovascular function, digestion, sexual function and so on. This is the part of the brain therefore which controls our entire endocrine and autonomic nervous system and mediates all our emotional expression. For any experience to be processed into memory then it must of necessity, because of the way we are structured, activate this system. It is thus through the emotions which we experience in our body that we know the significance of what is happening to us.

What the neurophysiologists don't tell us and what I am putting forward as a hypothesis, is that when, for example a child is faced with an overwhelming traumatic experience, the processing of this through the primitive brain can be blocked and never gets into memory. The experience is stored in its raw state almost like a video of the original happening and remains suspended, outside of time. I am suggesting this on the basis of the clinical evidence we see when working with those who have been severely traumatised. This would seem to be the only way in such circumstances that the child can survive. As the author points out the traumatic experience lies in wait perhaps to be activated many years later. In the meantime, particularly if there is continuous abuse, as Pierre Janet pointed out a hundred years ago, the only way in which the child can survive is to dissociate so that a whole dimension of the personality goes underground and the person may then have no awareness that these things have ever happened.

The practical importance of what I am putting forward is that, when some event later in life activates this suspended experience the processing of it into memory literally takes up from the point where it has been blocked and the person experiences the trauma (with all its physical and emotional concomitants) as happening *now*. It is this devastatingly confusing experience that the author is referring to when she says people often feel as if they are going mad. It is that feeling of something horrendous happening to us *now*, physically and emotionally, and yet intellectually knowing there is nothing taking place in the outside world to account for this which is so disturbing. I feel it is essential that we understand this correctly and realise that although the experience may relate to events which took place many years ago in childhood we are never actually dealing with the past, we are dealing with what is there now, the 'present' in its suspended state.

To my mind it is this fact, which makes the various stages Ms. Daniel describes the traumatised person having to go through, so important. I think it is the clear and unequivocal way in which she describes these that will make this book so valuable. I would certainly like to have it to give to clients who are going through this painful process, to read, and use as a workbook, and I believe it would be a very valuable support to them in facing what they have to face if they are ever to be healed.

I would strike one note of caution however in regard to a book of this kind, or to others such as *The Courage to Heal.* It has recently become clear from the work of over enthusiastic therapists how vigilant and careful we will have to be from now on if we are not fall into the trap of suggesting to clients (who may present with symptoms of depression, anxiety and so on), that these are due to traumatic experiences in childhood which in fact may never have happened. It is quite clear now that patients with unstable and borderline personalities are very open to suggestion of this kind.

Where genuine unassimilated traumatic experience presents spontaneously there is, in my experience, no doubt about its truth and accuracy. Indeed in many cases through relatives and others it has been possible to verify the genuineness of such experiences which emerged during therapy. In these genuine cases, far from the person being open to suggestion, it is usually a difficult struggle, as the author points out, to get them to face the pain and truth of what actually did happen. It is simply that from now on we must be very careful not to get in the position of leading the client or suggesting to them what may have happened. We should rather follow them patiently, supporting them, as they struggle to open up exquisitely painful experiences which have lain suspended in cold storage for many years.

Dr. Ivor Browne

THE BEGINNING

The lawns are full of violets today,
Blue and purple splashes in the green
Of deep-sprung grass. Forgotten is the gray
Of cold, indifferent winter, and the lean
And careful husbanding of hope. We wake
To sudden springtime, find ourselves caressed
With scent and blossom, watch the branches take
The growth of leaves. Is no one then distressed
At winter's loss? Does no one mourn the fine
Restraint and discipline of cold, regret
The wantonness of green that blurs the line
Of cool intent? No looking back: we let
The springtime come because we know we must,
Despite those bruises blooming in the dust.

A Note To The Reader

I wrote this book to help people who were brutalized in childhood. It is designed as a handbook to supplement whatever therapies, self-help programs or other courses of healing you are using as you work to free yourself of the nightmare of the past, and build a future free of terror and abuse.

The book is concise. It will not take long to read through it; carrying out its suggestions is what will take time and effort. In order to heal, you have to have help. A good therapist or counsellor is essential. But you are the key to your own healing. This book will give you a resource which you can use to speed your transformation.

CAUTION: This book was written for use by people who have actual trauma in their backgrounds which needs to be healed. Do not attempt to heal buried trauma without the assistance of a qualified professional. Any use of the concepts in this book to punish, harass or humiliate family members or acquaintances is unethical, unwise, and will not lead to healing. The concepts and techniques in this book represent the opinion of the author and should in no way be taken as absolute.

Part One:

Beginnings

If you were sexually abused as a child or tortured as an infant, chances are you won't remember it. In order to survive in your family, you had to forget what happened and how you felt about it, and you had to absorb your family's version of reality, lies and all.

Years later, the healing process begins with what seems to be disaster.

It usually starts after you make a break with the way you used to do things. You move out of your parents' home, or divorce an abusive spouse, quit drinking, or resign your job to start your own business. Or you fall in love with someone who opens your heart.

At first, everything seems fine; you've freed yourself from what you thought was holding you back. You've stood up for yourself. You've gone after something you wanted.

Then the chaos begins. It could be nightmares. It could be chronic fatigue, major illness, deep depression, mood swings, or flashbacks that throw you to your knees.

Life goes mad. You think you're going mad.

Then, by chance, you come across the idea of childhood abuse. You may have heard about child abuse several hundred times in your life with no personal reaction, but this time is different.

Something shifts inside. The adventure begins.

It won't feel like an adventure most of the time. It will upend your whole past, show you things you never wanted to know or remember about your family, and change your personality. It will feel dreadful more often than not.

And yet, it is an adventure and a journey to freedom.

This book is written to help you keep your head clear about what is happening to you and what you have to do to complete the healing process.

The next section lists what has to be done. I have kept the list itself simple, because in the chaos of your healing process, it's easy to forget the basics, as you will see.

After we've looked at what has to be done, we can talk about what sorts of activities can help you, how to recognize when you're stalling your own healing, and how to get past the barriers that come up.

This is an adventure worth doing. It is the most difficult thing you will ever do. Once you've come out the other side, you'll see that it's also the most valuable gift you have ever given yourself.

PART TWO:

WHAT HAS TO BE DONE

Here is the list of what you have to do to heal yourself. The list goes in rough chronological order, although you will find yourself moving back and forth from task to task as new layers of events and feelings emerge.

Whenever you feel stuck and think you're getting nowhere, return to this list. These things are very hard to do. It's easy to try to avoid them, easy to forget them. When you get stuck, there's a good chance it's because you're avoiding doing one of these things. (Don't waste time criticizing yourself for not wanting to do them. Who would want to do them? They're just necessary.)

1. Remember What Happened.
2. Tell Somebody.
3. Feel the Feelings.
4. Recognize Who Was Responsible.
5. Confront the Abuser.
6. Evaluate your Progress.

1

Remembering What Happened

Before you can heal the wounds inflicted on you by your family or other abusers, you have to remember what was done to you, and by whom.

This remembering is partly intellectual, partly emotional, and partly physical. Any of the three parts can be the first to emerge, but the remembering isn't complete until all three parts are present.

When I say you have to remember what was done to you, that doesn't mean, necessarily, that you have to recall dates, times, how many times it was done, how many years it continued, what was said before or after. Some people, gifted or cursed with total recall, will bring up everything. The rest of us will come up with some generalities and some specifics.

The importance of the remembering is to recognize what was done and by whom, and to know it's true that it happened.

It is common, in this remembering phase, to go through a lot of disbelief. Part of you will be saying, "This happened to me." Another part of you will be insisting, "Nobody does that to a child! That couldn't happen in MY family!" If you find that sort of division in yourself, just keep asking yourself what happened and it will eventually come clear.

2

Telling Somebody

One of the biggest tabus placed on the abused child is against telling anybody what was done and who did it. (No abuser wants it known.)

An almost universal feeling during the healing of the abuse is that you don't dare tell anybody. In fact, you won't heal unless you do tell.

Whom to tell is a question you have to decide for yourself. The only rule I would propose is that if the abuser was one of your family, you not tell anybody in your family in the first stages of the healing. Families that produce an abuser are not healthy, and the last thing you need now is more abuse from your family. Tell somebody you trust.

3

Feeling the Feelings

You need to recover the feelings that were buried inside you when you were abused, and you need to express them. The feelings are intense – sorrow, outrage, abandonment, rage, fear, loneliness, despair.

In unhealthy families, children are taught that it is dangerous even to have such emotions, let alone to express them, so you may feel as though you'll die if you allow yourself to know how you felt back then.

The truth is that you won't be healed at all unless you recover those emotions IN CONTEXT – feel again how you felt when you were abused, know the abuse as the source of the suffering and express what you feel.

It may take a long time to work your way through all the layers of hurt and anger you've been holding inside all these years. It's natural to be a coward about feeling them. But you'll walk around half healed unless you persist, and living half healed is living in hell. It's better to finish than to get stuck in the middle.

4

Recognising Who was Responsible

The biggest lie perpetrated by abusers of children is that the child is to blame for the abuse.

Child abusers are by definition irresponsible human beings. They will do and say anything to keep from knowing what they're actually doing to the child. Blaming the child is the perfect defense against inner knowledge of their own responsibility.

The lie works because children tend to blame themselves for anything that goes wrong in the family. They blame themselves for divorce. They blame themselves when somebody dies. There are even indications that the fetus will blame itself if it is uncomfortable in the womb. When they are tortured, beaten, sexually molested, children will blame themselves and will carry through their lives a deep inner conviction that they are bad.

To heal yourself of the damage done when you were abused, you have to look at the situation as it actually happened, and realize that it was the abuser who was responsible for the abuse, not you.

The lie of your guilt has affected how you see yourself and how you see your family. Overturning that lie will turn your past upside down, which is an uncomfortable experience. But exposing the lie as a lie is the only way you can stop punishing yourself for something you never did.

5

CONFRONTING THE ABUSER

In order to heal, you have to confront the person who abused you. You have to say what the abuse was, show that you know the abuser was at fault for what happened, and express your outrage that you were abused.

You need to do this in order to learn to stand up for yourself, to change the structure of how you relate to the world, to claim your freedom.

You don't have to confront your abuser in person. You can do it in writing. If your abuser is dead, you need to make a symbolic confrontation in order to free yourself. (See the next section for suggestions about how to do that.)

You may feel when you read this that confronting your abuser is the last thing you could ever do. You were taught to excuse your family for anything they did to you, so you will want to 'fix' this problem all by yourself. You can't. If you are to heal, you have to confront the person who damaged you.

6

Evaluate your Progress

If you can sense a positive change after doing the first five steps, then you're on the road to healing and only need to persist.

If you feel no relief and no positive change, there are at least two possibilities.

Possibility One: A family that produces one child abuser can produce more than one. If you have gone through all five steps to healing your wounds and find that you are still torturing yourself, still obsessed with having been abused, you may be protecting a second family member. Take another look at your childhood, find what you're trying not to remember, and go through the list of steps again.

Possibility Two: You're working on the wrong problem. If you have gone through all five steps and you feel crazier and more out of control and less and less happy, especially if you are eager to remember abuse and eager to confront, and yet find no relief or positive change in your life – then there is a strong possibility that you are working on the wrong issue. If abuse is not what is causing your difficulties, then working on abuse will not solve your difficulties. Only working on the real issue will bring healing. It is up to you to find out what that issue is.

1. Remember What Happened.
2. Tell Somebody.
3. Feel the Feelings.
4. Recognize Who Was Responsible.
5. Confront the Abuser.
6. Evaluate your Progress.

Part Three

Remembering – Hints and Patterns

If you're having trouble remembering what happened to you in childhood, one of your best resources will be the patterns in your life as it is now.

In some mysterious way, early abuse marks the victim for further abuse of the same kind. Look at your life as it has been as an adult, and see what events and relationships have bothered you the most. In each of them is a pattern of how you were treated as a child and how you responded to that treatment.

The pattern can be as obvious as having lovers who beat you up, or as subtle as not being able to keep your belongings organized. Each part of your life which tortures your heart and seems unchangeable can be a pointer to early abuse – and can be changed, when the abuse or other trauma is uncovered and dealt with.

Start with the more obvious problems. Look at the pattern of repetition. Avoid judging yourself – having had a string of bad lovers or abusive employers doesn't mean you 'want' to be abused. (What it usually means is that you don't recognize when you're being abused.) Just look at the event and allow yourself to feel your emotions. Then go back further in time until you find the first time it happened, or the first relationship that was like that.

The symptoms I have described can be caused by child abuse, but they can also have other causes. So it is vital that you be as open-minded as possible when you explore these patterns and clues to your past. Trust yourself to find the truth. You are the bearer of your own truth, and you will find it by persisting courageously. Only the truth will permit you to heal. Only you can find that truth.

More Clues – The Other Side of the Coin

Perhaps you can find none of the above in your life pattern, but still FEEL that you were abused. It may be that you have taken a different path from the one I outlined above. Other indications that you may have been severely abused in childhood or infancy are:

A persistent feeling that Men, or Women, or 'People,' OWE YOU something. Chances are somebody does, but it may not be the person you're trying to collect from.

Abusing other people. If you find yourself beating your children, sexually interfering with someone who is less powerful than you are, or verbally battering people for no obvious reason, you may be reenacting something which was done to you when you were weak and vulnerable. Stop doing it. Think about why you do it. 'Punishing' the weak is not a way to leave abuse behind – but it can be a clue that there was abuse which you suffered which needs to be healed.

The symptoms I have just described can be caused by having been abused, but they can also have other causes. It is very important to you and to those near to you that you find out what is behind these attitudes and behaviours. You are the bearer of your own truth, and you will find it by persisting courageously. Only the truth will permit you to heal. You are responsible for finding that truth.

Cleaning Up Your Present Relationships

The patterns set up in your childhood will have affected what you can tolerate in behavior from your friends. Once you begin discovering and healing what happened to you as a child, all your present friendships will be affected. People whom you thought would always support you may suddenly attack you for digging up the past. And people whose company you used to enjoy may suddenly seem abusive or boring or negative to you.

This is a chance to begin 'cleaning house' and standing up for yourself. The friends whom you gathered around you in the past were not relating to the new you who is on a quest for healing. They may turn out to be inappropriate friends for you once you open up childhood issues and begin feeling your pain.

Take care of yourself. No matter how long you have known somebody, you can't afford to have a lot of negativity, undermining and abuse in your life. You're too vulnerable at this point. You deserve to have love and support. If a friend begins to mistreat you or make you feel worthless, confront the friend, or drop the relationship, as you choose. You come first.

Dread of Confrontation

The most fearsome task in healing child abuse is confronting the abuser. It is the one thing all of us would put off until the end of time, if we could get away with it. Just thinking about making the confrontation reduces us to the terrified, helpless child who couldn't prevent the abuse in the first place.

And then, there are all those years when we pretended it never happened, wasn't important. What horrible things will happen if I do this? Everything combines to argue against confrontation, and yet it must be done.

The relationship you have had with your abuser is the single most powerful force hindering your healing. That relationship with the abuser is your mortal enemy. It has to be transformed. The only way to transform it is through confrontation.

When I say the relationship has to be transformed, I don't mean that you and your abuser have to live happily ever after, together. What I mean is that you have to change your own side of the relationship – take your power back, stand up for your right to feel, to perceive, to know the truth and to speak the truth.

Once you do that, you transform the relationship and your own future. It doesn't matter what the abuser's response is to the confrontation.

When you make the confrontation, you are not doing it in order to change the abuser. Chances are, the abuser will never change. So if you go at it wanting to punish or manipulate the abuser, or wanting to be happy together, you'll fail – wait until you can simply state your position and stick by it. That's all that's necessary.

If you are too afraid to make a confrontation, practice doing it by writing it down, role–playing it, saying it to an empty chair, painting or drawing it, and by standing up for yourself in other circumstances. Practice until you get your courage up, and then make your confrontation. A good therapist can make all the difference in helping you to prepare for a confrontation.

Once you've done it, you will probably go through a time of feeling that you have done wrong to be so rude to this person who 'loves' you. That's a normal hangover from your early training, and it's the exact opposite of the truth. In fact, the more dread you feel after having confronted your abuser, the more likely it is that you have done exactly the right thing for yourself. Remind yourself of what the person did to you and to your life. Stand by your truth.

1. Remember What Happened.
2. Tell Somebody.
3. Feel the Feelings.
4. Recognize Who Was Responsible.
5. Confront the Abuser.
6. Evaluate your Progress.

If Your Abuser is Dead

If your abusers have died before you discovered what they did to you, the good news is that you won't be running into them at the supermarket. The bad news is that you have no one to confront directly.

You can make a confrontation with a dead abuser by writing it out and reading it at the abuser's grave, by reading it to someone who agrees to stand in for the abuser, by reading it to an empty chair which you have designated the abuser.

You can also confront a dead abuser through living family members. You tell somebody who was close to the person what was done to you, who did it, how it made you feel, how outraged you are, etc. Because families that produce an abuser tend to have a lot of other abusers, enablers, codependents and deniers, you will be confronting the same forces which produced the abuse.

Balancing Anger and Sorrow

When you allow yourself to feel your emotions about the abuse that happened to you, the most important emotions involved will be anger and sorrow. Depending on your temperament, you will tend to favor one or the other.

It is important for your healing that you balance your response. People who get stuck in anger have tantrums to avoid feeling their sorrow. People who never get angry use sorrow as a mask for despair instead of activating their anger. As you explore your emotions, exercise both anger and sorrow, even if you have to stimulate one of them somewhat artificially.

If you work and work on this task and still get stuck in the anger or the sorrow, and especially if you never get better and only get worse from working on it, it may be that you are working on the wrong issue – the wrong incident, the wrong trauma, or somebody else's idea of what happened to you rather than what really happened. Working on false memories won't heal you; working on real ones will.

Releasing Emotions

When you have felt your emotions in the context of the abuse and expressed them in some way, you need to let them go. That means opening them up and letting them sort themselves out without trying to 'fix' the conflict by explaining it away.

Let's say, for instance, that your father raped and beat you. You realize that: A. you loved your father and trusted him, B. he told you he loved you, and C. he attacked and damaged you. To release the emotions of that situation, let yourself feel all sides of it at the same time. Avoid trying to lessen the pain by saying, "I was an idiot to have loved him if he did that," or "he must have loved me because he said he did," or "how could I have been so stupid not to know what was happening," or any other sentence that would deny part of the situation.

It's painful to feel all those conflicting emotions. But if you just let the emotions BE, without making judgements about them or trying to explain them away, over a period of a few days they will begin to evaporate and the pain of the conflict will resolve itself without your having to force it into any particular shape.

Feel it all. Imagine yourself opening it up – to the Universe, to God, to the air, whatever works for you – and let it be. It will radiate out of you and resolve itself. As with any part of this healing, you may have to go back again to release other emotions about other situations. Don't think you're stuck if you have to repeat things – we all do.

The Issue of Forgiveness

Forgiveness is very important in healing from abuse, but it is not on my list of things to do in order to heal. The reason for my not including it is that the concept of forgiveness is a dangerous one for people who have been abused, and it has been misused by those who try to help abused people to heal.

Ideally, you will eventually remove all traces of the abuse in your heart and be free of it forever, no longer hampered by its effects, at peace with your own life history and benevolent toward others, including your abuser. This is forgiveness. It is a goal, but it is also a product of giving up abuse in all its forms, which is what you will have done through using this book, through participating in therapy and counseling. Forgiveness is the end result of leaving abuse behind.

But when it comes to forgiving the perpetrator of violence to you while you are still in the process of freeing yourself from the effects of the violence, there is a big danger. Abused children have been forced again and again to overlook what has happened to them. They have been in a position of no power in a brutal world. They have been taught that they have no rights. They don't know what forgiveness is – they only know submission. So when victims of child abuse are told that they have to forgive in order to heal, what they will do is submit instead. They will assume they are wrong to have their feelings of outrage and anger, and will hand over their power once again to the abuser. Instead of healing, they will be caught in the traps of denial and submission.

Forgiveness is a concept so confused and misapplied that it has great peril for the victim of child abuse. Victims of child abuse don't need to be taught to forgive; they need to be taught to stand up for themselves.

This is true also of the concept of forgiving yourself. Forgiving implies that there is some offense to be forgiven. Yes, of course, if you are attacking and abusing other people you have to take responsibility for your behavior, get to the root of it, change your attitude and make amends where you can. That involves forgiving yourself for your bad deeds. But to 'forgive' yourself for 'allowing' yourself to be abused as a child is inappropriate because you weren't responsible for the abuse. Realizing that you were not at fault is vital – 'forgiving' yourself can be a trap which convinces you that in fact you were at fault. Concentrate on getting yourself healed, and the forgiveness will take care of itself.

Taking Charge of your Truth

Just as it is the abuser's responsibility for having abused you, it is now – unfair though it may seem – your own responsibility to take charge of your life and of your healing. Friends can help. Therapists can help. But you are the key to your own healing, and it is your responsibility to find the truth of your past. Don't allow anybody to suggest that abuse happened to you, and don't allow anybody to suggest that abuse did *not* happen to you. Be willing to listen to other people, but be aware that your memories are *your* memories and that your life is *your* life. Child abuse is a subject which arouses all sorts of irrational responses in people. The people who are helping you are not immune to irrationality. They're just human, after all, as we all are. You find your truth, and you stand by your truth. It's your own life you're dealing with. It is your own healing that is at stake.

THE ISSUE OF REVENGE

Taking revenge for what was done to you, whether by doing violence to an abuser or by humiliating him/her, or by claiming legal damages, will not heal you. Becoming obsessed by the desire for revenge will keep you locked in the cycle of abuse. Confrontation is necessary; taking revenge is a big step backward. If you find yourself obsessed with revenging yourself for what was done to you, go back to the list and do everything again. Chances are, you are burying anger and not facing the truth of what happened. Open it up and discharge it. It is your healing which is at stake, not the fate of your abuser. Remember that each abuser is repeating, on an innocent victim, what was done to her/him by somebody else. If you get stuck in anger and vengefulness, you may not become a child abuser, but you will not heal.

Choosing a Therapist

A good therapist is beyond price. You'll need one who can deal with sexual abuse. There is no guarantee from a person's credentials alone that he or she has those skills, but you can figure it out in person.

The best way to sense it is by bringing up the subject with your prospective therapist and watching his/her reactions. If the prospective therapist shows any sign of attacking or demeaning you or failing to believe you, this is not the helper you need. If your concerns are treated with respect and support, you're on the right track.

As a formerly abused person, you are particularly vulnerable to authority figures who promise to 'fix' the problem, or who stand in for your abusers in some way. If at any time you feel that your therapist is trying to make you dependent or keep you weak, bring the subject out in the open immediately. A good therapist will be able to show his/her trustworthiness; a bad one will waffle on the issues.

The therapist is there for you as a resource – someone outside your situation who can suggest helpful alternatives. If you get any sense that your therapist is: 1. Badmouthing other therapies or therapists, 2. Suggesting memories to you that feel untrue, or 3. Egging you on to sue someone, begin immediately to question her/his character and motives. You can change therapists. It's allowed!

Many people who were tortured or abused developed what might be called paranormal abilities, just in order to survive. If things were very dangerous emotionally in your home, you may have learned how to feel other people's feelings, so you'd know when to duck or disappear. You may have learned how to disappear when an emotional storm was brewing, or when you needed some time alone.

As you become more mature and break away from your past somewhat, these abilities may suddenly increase.

Because our present society is so rationalistic, it may be difficult to find guidance when unusual abilities surface. There are many, many paths to such help, and you will find them. Keep in mind, though, that just as you are vulnerable to the therapist who has a bad character, you are also vulnerable to any 'New Age' practitioner whose unconscious motivation is the exploitation of power from his/her students or disciples.

Patience and Persistence

As I mentioned earlier, the list of things that has to be done in order to heal is very short – very short, and very difficult to do. As you work your way through the list, back and forth as necessary, you will be opening up new parts of yourself, or old parts of yourself which were locked away in childhood. Your personality and your way of living in the world will change. Some of the changes may be very uncomfortable. If you've always looked on the bright side, for instance, it will be a shock to enter a time when all you see is what you don't like. Have patience with yourself. The bad will pass. And once it does, your life will be transformed. This transformation is the greatest service you can do for yourself. Have patience. Persist. Healing is there for you.

1. Remember What Happened.
2. Tell Somebody.
3. Feel the Feelings.
4. Recognize Who Was Responsible.
5. Confront the Abuser.
6. Evaluate your Progress.

Necessary Travel

It's light again, mornings,
going to work. Not long ago
rising was in darkness and only
at arrival did the mirrored buildings
flash the news of coming day –
a silent glory seen by the few of us
awake enough to notice.

Rising was in darkness; going home,
the same – with bulky figures crowding
the platform, doing what they must
to make the trip.

By now, to see that early mirrored flash
I would have to travel long before my body
is ready to leave its sleep – or
stay awake to watch for secret dawn.

I travel by daylight now, both ways;
the year moves on.

The light is here, and now we take it
for granted, grumbling a bit at the cold,
wanting summer, teased by this sun
which gives its promise, yet leaves us
restless, wanting more warmth, more time, more joy,
more of something – more of everything.

But we may as well be patient, saved as we've been
so recently from rising in the night;
The weather always lags behind the light.